AS MAMA USED TO SAY

Like her mother, Kathy Kuczka has a nose for news and a heart directed toward the divine. An award-winning journalist, she spent many years covering news for *CNN*. In demand as a writer and speaker, Kathy is a frequent contributor to various publications covering travel, religion and the performing arts. She received a BA in Communications from Hofstra University and an MA in Religious Studies from the Catholic University of America. She is a liturgy director in the Archdiocese of Atlanta. In her spare time, she sings and acts in theaters throughout Atlanta.

Kathy is pictured above with her mother, Violanda, and her brother, John.

As Mama Used to Say

Life Lessons Learned from
a Mother's Mottoes

KATHY KUCZKA

ST PAULS

Library of Congress Cataloging-in-Publication Data

Kuczka, Kathy.
  As mama used to say: life lessons learned from a mother's mottoes /
Kathy Kuczka.
      pages cm.
  Includes bibliographical references and index.
  ISBN 978-0-8189-1376-1 (alk. paper)
  Kuczka, Kathy. 2. Conduct of life. 3. Mothers—Conduct of life. I. Title.
  BJ1589.K83 2014
  170'.44—dc23
                        2014038830

Produced and designed in the United States of America by the
Fathers and Brothers of the Society of St. Paul,
2187 Victory Boulevard, Staten Island, New York 10314-6603
as part of their communications apostolate.

ISBN 978-0-8189-1376-1

Current Printing - first digit   1   2   3   4   5   6   7   8   9   10

Place of Publication:
2187 Victory Blvd., Staten Island, NY 10314 - USA

Year of Current Printing - first year shown

2015 2016 2017 2018 2019 2020 2021 2022 2023 2024

Acknowledgments

To my Aunt Carolyn, who has been urging me to write a book since I was old enough to write and who has helped proofread this manuscript.

To my friend, author Robert Davis, for whose guidance and mentoring I will be forever grateful.

To Terry Zobel, friend, teacher, and counselor in all things spiritual, for reading this manuscript and making many helpful suggestions.

To my brother John Kuczka, who helped provide the words, the memories, and the stories in this book. He is a constant source of love and encouragement, and his kindness and generosity inspire me; I give thanks to God for him each and every day.

Table of Contents

Introduction

What is it about a mother's voice that sets it apart from all other voices? Even before we are born, our ears instinctively become attuned to the sound of our mother's voice. As we begin to learn how to speak, the words from our mother's lips seem to pierce through the clamor of other speech to become readily distinguishable. The impact from those words doesn't fade as we grow into adulthood. Those words are so deeply ingrained in us that they often resound in our own lives. The words or sayings of our mothers – some of which we vowed never to repeat – often find a stage for replay in the events and episodes of our adult lives. That is what this book is about – my mother's words – and my reflections on them.

My mother, Violanda Thomas, was born in the rural hills of western Pennsylvania in the town of New Castle, the daughter of Italian immigrants, Philomena Circelli-Thomas and Columbus Thomas. She changed her name to Violet, but everyone called her Vi.

She married my father in 1960 and had two children, my brother John and me.

My mother wasn't perfect, but like most mothers, she usually claimed that she was right. And, most of the time she was. Mom died in 1996, yet she remains alive in so many ways: in personality traits now visible in her children, in family traditions handed down for generations, and in her words of wisdom gleaned from an often difficult but well-lived life.

Each chapter in this book takes its title from one of my mother's cherished sayings. The chapters in this book are short, but the wisdom they convey can take a lifetime to ponder. It is my hope that this book will demonstrate how reflecting on our mothers' axioms, aphorisms, and adages can offer simple but profound wisdom that can help us better live out our adult lives.

Some of the phrases may remind you of similar phrases your mother used to say; some you may find yourself repeating to your own children. Either way, I believe that you, like me, will discover that a mother's voice has sustaining power. The seeds of wisdom harvested from a mother's favorite sayings will never go out of style. In an age where children are barraged by the images and the influence of multiple media platforms, it's nice to know a mother's human voice still has value – even years later.

Like a tune I can't get out of my head, my mother's voice is always there, awakening and admonishing, challenging and affirming me. Since I have no children of my own, I am passing on my mother's sayings and her wisdom to you. It is my hope that you, too, might be as awakened and admonished, challenged and affirmed by her words as I have been.

Do not forsake your mother's teachings.

Bind them upon your heart always;

Tie them around your neck.

When you walk, they will lead you;

When you lie down, they will watch
over you;

And when you awake, they will talk
with you.

(Proverbs 6:20–23)

1

Say your prayers

Prayer was part of the daily routine at our house. We prayed before supper and every now and then we would pray the rosary together. Prayer was also part of the nightly regimen. Before she went to sleep, I would see Mom kneeling at the side of her bed saying her prayers. She would pray the rosary and/or read out of a book called *Mother Love*, a book of prayers written for Christian wives and mothers. Whenever I woke up in the middle of the night and couldn't get back to sleep, Mom would whisper, "Say your prayers." Mom knew about the power of prayer. Sometimes, I think it was the only thing that held her together. She had come to depend on the grace of God as a baby depends on a parent. She relied on the power of God to empower her throughout the day. Because of her prayer life, she imaged God as a faithful companion and intimate friend. She spoke as if she and God were on a first-name basis. Prayer became the foundation of her faith, a foundation that was never shaken.

When she died, my foundation was shaken and the last thing I wanted to do was to pray. I was angry and I felt spiritually paralyzed. Not long after my mother's death, I had lunch with one of my graduate school professors. I told her about my inability to pray. She said to me, "God can handle your anger much more than God can handle your silence."

My professor gave me the courage I needed to begin anew. At the start, all I could pray were these words: *I'm angry.* Somehow that was enough to begin to chip away the walls of my own bitterness. I realized that the times when we want to pray the least are the times when we need to pray the most. Perhaps these are the times when prayer is most powerful – when we come before God with raw emotions, naked and vulnerable, stripped of our ego, baring our soul and daring to hope. Even uttering the word *why?* is a powerful prayer. When we say anything in prayer, even if it is one word, we assume some-one is listening. That is hope. That hope gives us the strength to move forward.

As I moved forward with my grief, I dis-covered a lot about prayer. To pray is not to bow our heads so low and fold our hands so tight that we close in on ourselves, but rather to open our arms and to lift our faces as if we are anticipating a shower of grace. To pray is to empty ourselves of ourselves so that we can be filled with God's very self. Prayer helps us to form and maintain a relationship with God. Prayer is not about getting God to listen to us; it's about getting us to listen to God. It's not about getting God to see things our way; it's about get-ting us to see things God's way. Prayer changes things. Prayer changes us. As my mom taught, prayer is not something we do only when we want something. Prayer is a way of life.

2

Watch this! This is history!

There is something about history in the making that is so riveting and so invigorating that it etches itself into our memory. That's why we can remember with clarity where we were when the most significant events in history took place. We may not be able to remember what we had for lunch yesterday, but we can remember where we were and what we were doing when President John F. Kennedy was assassinated on November 22, 1963, or when the Twin Towers and the Pentagon were attacked on September 11, 2001. Whenever historic events were being broadcast live, Mom was glued to the television and she encouraged us to do the same, saying, "Watch this. This is history."

On July 20, 1969, we were at our grandmother's house watching Walter Cronkite and retired Astronaut Wally Schirra cover the space-flight that landed the first humans on the moon. Mom wouldn't let us leave until we witnessed Neil Armstrong's first step onto the moon's sur-face some hours after the spaceflight landed. When the feet of "Eagle" touched down, Schirra wiped a tear from his eye and Cronkite took his glasses off and said, "Say something, Wally, I'm speechless." It's that kind of awe that drew Mom into watching these historic events and she wanted her children to share the experience. Not all historic events were as inspiring as the first man on the moon. Some are disheartening. One such event was the Watergate scandal and the subsequent resignation of President Richard Nixon on August 9, 1974. Those events were both sad and fascinating at the same time.

History takes our emotions on a thrill ride as we experience the highs and the lows of living via the stories of other people. We felt the courage of the "tank man" on June 5,

1989, when he attempted to stop a cavalcade of Chinese tanks a day after the Chinese military cracked down on protestors in Tiananmen Square. We were filled with horror when hundreds of thousands of Rwandans were killed in 1994 in a mass slaughter. We were exhilarated by the underdog 1980 U.S. Olympic Hockey Team when they defeated their opponents, the powerful Soviet squad, and then went on to win the gold medal. We cried with those who lost loved ones when Hurricane Katrina unleashed its fury on the Gulf Coast in 2005.

Mom's fascination with history prompted me to go into journalism. As a news writer at CNN, I was able to cover major historic events such as the fall of the Berlin Wall and the collapse of the Cold War, all because Mom encouraged me to watch history as it unfolded.

History gives us the prism through which to view the multifaceted colors of human beings, showing us how humans act and react. History exposes humanity in its shadow and in its light.

It teaches us what to embrace and what to avoid. Mom not only wanted us to watch history as it unfolded on television, she wanted us to learn from it. As the philosopher George Santayana said, "Those who cannot learn from history are doomed to repeat it."

3

Don't make it too heavy

It was a Saturday ritual – going to the grocery store – usually after my mother had her weekly Saturday morning hair appointment. My mother had a way of hitting almost every store in town. There was Joseph's Supermarket for produce, Berkley's Meat Market for meat, and Giant Eagle for everything else. Going to the grocery store to pick up a few things usually turned into a half-day shopping spree. I guess she wanted to spread the wealth.

That was in the 1960s and 70s, when the question, "Is plastic OK?" wasn't even on the radar of most grocery marketing managers. When Mom and I would get to the cashier, she would say to the bagger, "Don't make it too heavy." She knew that she and I would have to carry the bags from the store to the car and then from the car to the house, and in western Pennsylvania, that could have meant in the kind of ice and snow which are only appreciated by winter Olympians. I didn't realize it at the time, but "Don't make it too heavy" was a metaphor for my mother's life. Raising two children as a single mother wasn't easy. It was as if she was reminding herself, "I can only carry so much."

I grew up wanting to be an actress. I took advantage of every opportunity in school to get stage experience: speech contests, talent shows, plays and musicals. But I learned at an early age that competition was tight. There were usually a lot more people than available roles. But one summer there was an announcement to audition for a musical at an outdoor amphitheater in a nearby town. I was so excited about the possibility. It would be a dream come true, I remember thinking. But it would mean my mother would have to drive me back and forth to rehearsals and performances. A vehement "no" was my mother's answer when I asked if I could audition. I was devastated. It was as if she threw ice on the flame inside of me. Didn't she realize how much the experience would mean to me? Didn't she know that I needed as much exposure as possible? Later I realized that my mother wasn't attempting to squash my dreams or thwart my future. My mother was merely preserving her energy, and therefore our family by affirming to herself, "I can only carry so much." My mother knew she couldn't carry it all. She knew when enough was enough and when to ask for help.

Years later, when I was in Sydney for the 2000 Summer Olympics, I took a side trip to the Blue Mountains. Our guide told many legends and lore about the indigenous people of Australia, the Aborigines. Aborigines lived as hunter-gatherers, hunting and gathering food from the land. According to our guide, the Aboriginal people had a saying, "If you can't carry it, you don't need it." The Aborigines not only lived by this statute, it became the core of their survival. The Aborigines had no shopping bags, paper, plastic or otherwise. They had to rely only on what their arms could carry. They had to trust that what they could carry would be enough to sustain them.

The wisdom of my mother and the Aboriginal Australians poses many challenges. How often do we carry more than we need? There is always one more thing to buy, one more activity in which to participate, one more "yes" to something we have neither time for nor interest in. There is also the emotional baggage we carry – the hurts that we can't let go, the vengefulness we hold prey and the grief that prevents us from moving on. If we reminded ourselves, "I can only carry so much," the heaviness of life just might result in a lighter way of living.

4

Did you send a thank-you note?

My mother was big on saying thank you. Most of her gratitude came in the form of baked goods – scrumptious edibles like homemade Easter bread or apple squares. She offered these mouth-watering treats to those who constantly showed kindness to us – Dr. John Prioletti, our family doctor, who never took a penny after our father died, or the neighbors who plowed our driveway after massive snowfalls. Mom recognized goodness in the hearts of others and was eternally grateful. By focusing on the blessings rather than the pain of life, she often changed those potentially painful moments into moments of thanksgiving.

Years ago, I traveled to Ireland with a correspondent, a camera person, and an audio technician to cover travel stories for CNN. Our enthusiasm was bubbling over as we sailed across the Irish Sea to Belfast. Our first few days were spent in Northern Ireland. We were awed with the beauty of the Antrim coast, overwhelmed by the hospitality of the people, and astonished by their history. Stupefied by the stupendous castles and lured by the luscious green landscapes, our camera crew couldn't wait to start rolling. After more than a week of working long-hour days, our enthusiasm started to wane. As the country became more familiar, the newness wore off and our initial excitement faded. The coastal beauty seemed to have lost some of its glimmer. The emerald countryside appeared a little less striking. Even the castles seemed less spectacular. In the final days of the trip, there were times when we had to practically beg our photographers to get a few shots.

Life is often like that trip. The longer we stay in one place, one job, or one relationship, the greater the challenge to sustain our initial passion and fervor. Honeymoons never last long enough. We long for newness, which soon becomes old. Then we complain that we're bored. And boredom often seduces us to take for granted all that we have been given.

Gratitude trounces the demons of despair. Gratitude triumphs over our tendencies to take life for granted. Gratitude shifts our focus and teaches us to hold each moment like a precious stone. Gratitude is the foundation of greatness. The greatest achievers in the history of human-kind know the importance of gratitude. They take *nothing* for granted. The greatest scientists understand that the tiniest particle of matter might hold the potential for the long-awaited cure. Virtuoso violinists know the slightest dif-ference in the curve of the thumb can enable the kind of performance that moves an audience to tears.

Ignatius of Loyola, saint and founder of the religious order known as the Jesuits, taught that gratitude gives us the newness for which we long, and it is there for the taking every day of our lives. His spiritual exercises include a daily examination of conscience that specifically focuses on gratitude. Step 2 of the *Examen* calls participants to look back over the past 24 hours and to remember those moments in the day for which they are grateful, be it for small things like the smell of morning coffee or a kind word someone uttered to larger encounters, such as an unexpected promotion or good news from a doctor. Gratitude compels us to widen the lens on our lives, to see the gifts we have been given, to know that there is a God who cares, to trust that life is unfolding – just as it should.

5

Red up this house because you never know who is coming!

People from Pittsburgh, Pennsylvania, and surrounding areas take pride in their own unique dialogue. The term *red up* is Pittsburghese for cleaning or tidying up. My mother was a neat freak. There was the living room that no one used, which included a sofa on which only guests were allowed to sit. Strangely enough, my mother would rearrange this furniture that no one used every so often to mark the change in seasons.

My brother and I were not messy kids. We would hang our clothes up in their respective closets or tuck them at least somewhat neatly away in their proper dresser drawers. Neatness was ingrained in us like a virtue and had all but become the 11th commandment. I had nightmares about strangers coming in the middle of the night with white gloves to inspect the dust on our bannisters. Still, my mother's proverb taught us to have our "house in order" just in case unexpected guests would show up at our doorstep. And, they did. My father's sister, my aunt Agnes, came often unannounced, neighbors popped in unexpectedly, as did numerous others whose cars ran into our mailbox in inclement weather.

My mother's vigilance about cleanliness, as attentive and as watchful as the parent of a newborn or a secret service agent, taught us the art of anticipation. It promised us that keeping our eyes wide open meant that we would ultimately see what we are looking for.

My brother John is into cars. Cars excite him, enthrall him, exhilarate him, and always have. Show him a picture of any car and he'll tell you the year, the make, the model, and a bit of the car's history. Classic cars really turn him on and he can spot them miles away. I'm reminded of this every time we're on the road. A routine drive often becomes a rousing reconnaissance mission. Gasps of excitement are followed by shouts of exclamation like, "Hey, there's a 1964 Shelby Cobra!" or, "Look! There's a 1973 Porsche 911RS!" My brother becomes once again like a little child, excited and filled with wonder. Against the backdrop of ordinary traffic, my brother's fascination with cars enables him to see the cars that other eyes might typically miss. But then again, he's always watching for them. The irony is, my brother can only see out of one eye.

What would happen if we all lived in a constant state of watchfulness? It seems if we were truly vigilant, we would not only anticipate life's surprises, we would also be well prepared for the inevitable circumstances of life. "Red up this house, you never know who is coming" taught us to anticipate, to expect, and to watch for life's surprises. "You never know" indeed.

6

God willing

Mom would typically follow almost everything that was said or respond to questions regarding future plans with the simple phrase, "God willing." Here are a couple examples: Mom: "Next weekend, we'll go bowling, God willing." Me: "Mom, can I go to Mary Ann's birthday party?" Mom: "God willing." For some reason, that always made me a little anxious. I thought, "Why wouldn't God want us to go bowling or go to Mary Ann's birthday party?" Every plan, every future moment was not set in stone at all, but seemed to be governed by an omnipotent being who held the yes or no card to each and every moment. For me, this formed an impression of God as a divine puppeteer, controlling our every move. I would think, "Doesn't God have more important things on the divine to-do list than to worry about my social calendar?" What exactly is God's will anyway? It's a question that occupied much of my childhood.

I was born with a bilateral cleft lip and palate. The defect runs in my family. I remember overhearing my mother telling one of my aunts the story of my birth. She said that after I came out of the womb the doctor told her and my father the news and then both she and Dad started to cry. Most births are accompanied by tears of joy. Mine came along with tears tinged with sadness, sobriety, fear of the unknown and anxiety about what the future might bring.

Growing up with any defect isn't easy, especially one that confronts you every time you look in the mirror. Strangers stared. Fellow classmates were cruel. And meeting new friends was difficult. I would often be interrogated with "What happened to your mouth?" That was only one half of the experience. There were also the zillions of doctor and dental appointments, doz-

ens of surgeries and endless sessions of counting
to 10 before speech therapists.

In all of this I wondered over and over
again, is this really God's will for me? Why did
God create me like this? Why does God will
that I suffer? How could an all-loving God cause
so much misery? Could I really believe in God
when I was in so much pain? Why? Why? Why?
I wanted answers – clear, black-and-white answers. And I wanted them immediately. I fooled
myself into thinking that the answers could take
away my pain or make me feel whole.

My unease came from the fact that I had
no control over my own genetics. It was out of
my hands. I was powerless in the fate of my own
destiny. My mother's constant "God willings"
were subtle but strong reminders that I was not
in charge, that there were parts of life that I didn't
get to choose. But as my mother helped me see,
I did have a choice. I could choose to accept
or to reject my reality. I could choose the way I
saw myself. I could choose how to react to the

way others saw me. And I could choose how I would view God, as nonexistent, or as a cosmic bully, or as a sacred spirit who only wills good.

I watched closely the choices my mother made. She chose to love me no matter what. She chose to focus on her children rather than on her own loneliness after our father died. She chose to go to great lengths to see that her daughter received the best care, driving long distances each month to Pittsburgh where my doctors were located. Every day, my mother was confronted with life's hardships. She changed what she could and surrendered the rest. She may have struggled with questions about God's will, but in the end she chose to trust God's love. She understood what it meant to live the Serenity Prayer, the prayer attributed to theologian Reinhold Niebuhr:

> *God, grant me the serenity to accept the*
> *things I cannot change,*
> *the courage to change the things I can and*
> *the wisdom to know the difference.*

God willing

Mom made me realize that the more I accepted myself and my life, the more peace I felt. The more I saw myself as an extension of a divine creation, the more joy I had. The more I saw God as willing abundant life, the more love I knew.

So what is God's will? As my mother helped me to see, there are no clear-cut answers. There is only life to be lived. Thanks to my mother, I will live it in peace, God willing.

7

Don't pay attention to him/her

I remember the day I started seventh grade. I was transferring to a large public school from a small Catholic school. I was excited but nervous. I had become comfortable with the conventions of my old school. I was accustomed to a certain routine, and I was relaxed around familiar friends and faces. That year, the teachers at my new school decided to strike. So on day one, instead of having classes, the student body gathered in the cafeteria. I walked in and there they were – 600 strange faces that seemed to be staring at me all at the same time. How would I get to know them? Would they like me? Would any of them become lifelong friends or merely remain acquaintances? Feelings of longing to be deeply immersed in this new community churned inside of me as I sat isolated and silent in the midst of a chirping crowd of peers who had known each other for years. I felt so alone. To make matters worse, a student in the eighth grade began making fun of me. His mockery shot through me like a knife. I wanted to crawl into a hole. After what seemed like an eternity, we boarded the buses home. I don't think I ever ran so fast. I couldn't wait to get home. My mother asked how the day went. In the midst of my tears, I told her about the mean boy in the eighth grade and what he did to me. "Don't pay attention to him" was her answer. "What?" I protested, "How could you just casually cast off my feelings as if they were nothing? Someone hurt me. That person was unfair. How could they have said that or done that to me?" I was annoyed and outraged.

My mother wasn't trying to be insensitive. She was teaching me a lesson about attention, a lesson that would come to light during my freshman year in college. My first year of higher academia was spent at the University of Pittsburgh in the thriving town of Oakland on the outskirts of the city. All freshmen took electives and psychology was one of mine. It was in that psychology class where the teacher said, "It is a proven fact that your mind cannot focus on more than one thing at a time."

My professor was right. His teaching brought me back to what happened during my first ride on a Ferris wheel. I was determined to ride the Ferris wheel but I was scared. Fear gripped me as I entered the platform and took my seat. I was with my Aunt Ann. When the operator pulled the arm to begin the ride, my heart was in my throat. That's when Aunt Ann started talking. She talked for the whole 4 minutes and 20 seconds of the ride and never stopped. She talked about family, and she asked me questions, which meant my mind was more engaged in conversation than on my fear. Before I knew it, the ride was over and I had survived. I actually enjoyed it and would go again and again, all because my aunt knew how to divert my attention.

Parents discover the art of diverting attention early on. Whether their children have a minor fall or a temper tantrum, they often say or do things that will redirect their children's attention. And within seconds a temper tantrum can become a laughing fit. My mother knew this art well. She taught me that where I put my attention mattered big-time! She showed me that focusing attention on certain people or situations gives them life, while not focusing attention on certain people or situations allows them to fade away peacefully. She taught me to focus my attention on the people and the things that really mattered. And, to her, an eighth-grade boy's opinion of her daughter's looks wasn't one of them.

8

He/She must not be a happy person

There is an old quip which describes two types of people: an optimist and a pessimist.

It goes like this: an optimist wakes up and says, "Good morning, God!" A pessimist wakes up and says, "Oh God, it's morning." An optimist sees the bright side of life and offers encouragement, confidence, inspiration, and reassurance. Being with an optimist is life-giving. An optimist is happy. A pessimist, on the other hand, sees the dark side of life and offers discouragement, cynicism, despair, doubt, gloom, and negativity. Being with a pessimist is draining. A pessimist is unhappy. While the attitudes of both optimists and pessimists have a huge influence on others, our human nature tends to be more impacted by the attitude of pessimists. After all, misery loves company, as they say. It's all too easy to get sucked into a downward spiral by the negative attitudes of other people, unless you are Violet Kuczka. Mom knew the root cause of negativity. When she, or my brother or I encountered those pessimists, she would say, "He/She must not be a happy person."

My years of hospital stays enabled me to encounter many people with other medical issues. I remember the morning of one particular surgery. I was lying outside my room in the hallway, ready to be taken to the operating room. I heard the voices of two persons who were also getting ready to journey to the O.R. They were twins, around 18 years old, who had been terribly burned and were awaiting their next plastic surgery. The burns had left them with gruesome facial scars, but they were talking, laughing, and carrying on as if they were going to a party instead of operating suite #3. I wondered how they could be so happy when they had suffered so much loss. Apparently, they had come to realize happiness on a whole other plane. Whatever they had I wanted.

They, like Mom, helped me realize that happiness is not about what we look like on the outside, it's how we view ourselves from the inside. Happiness is not about how much we have or how much we've accomplished. It's not about our social status or our social circles. While these things can add to our happiness, they can't *make* us happy. We fool ourselves into thinking that when we get the next job, relationship, house, and so on, that we will finally be happy. But life doesn't work that way. Happiness is fundamentally a choice. Some people, like the twins, come to understand this early on. But there are many who never discover this wisdom. To those persons, Mom's response, "He/She must not be a happy person," is one of understanding. She knew that some people will just never be happy and she felt compassion for them. Her wisdom and empathy have helped me to accept, rather than to reject the pessimists in my life, to examine the negative attitudes in my own heart, and to wake up each day and say, "Thank God, it's morning!"

9

*Everything is good
when you're hungry*

Mom was a fabulous cook and a terrific baker. She learned from her mother, who brought to this country the most delectable dishes from the kitchens and culture of her hometown in Italy. The smell of Mom's cooking always filled us with anticipation. No matter what was on the day's menu, our taste buds would dance for joy. My brother and I would often exclaim, "This is good!" Instead of accepting our compliments, Mom would say, "Everything is good when you're hungry." On the surface these words were true enough. But she said it so often I wondered if she was hinting at something more. In saying, "Everything is good when you're hungry," Mom was emphasizing our hunger rather than her culinary craftsmanship. She cared that we were hungry when we came to the table. She was even excited by it. Before we would sit down to eat she would ask with eagerness, "Are you hungry, honey?" In her own way, she was encouraging, affirming, even urging our hunger pangs – but why?

I discovered the answer when my jaw was wired shut for eight weeks. Everything I ate, or rather drank, as the case was, had to be blended into a fine liquid in order to fit through the maze of wires in my mouth. The savory smell of my mother's food wafting through the house nearly killed me. My family would be eating a juicy, scrumptious meal while I sat staring at my reflection in a bowl of clear chicken broth. Yet because I was so hungry, that broth tasted like fine dining. In fact, I was so hungry during that time that anything and everything was good, even a bowl of clear chicken broth! My mother was right! Everything *is* good when you're hungry. I learned how to survive with a meager portion and perhaps most important, how to be satisfied with what I had.

I've observed some important things about hunger. When we are hungry, we are filled with anticipation, longing, yearning, desiring, aspiring, and hoping. Hunger creates space for spiritual sustenance, something that ordinary food could never satisfy. Hunger can lead to solidarity with others who hunger, whether for daily bread or human dignity. This is part of the reason fasting is a key component in most religions, and perhaps the reason Jesus proclaimed those who hunger as blessed.

My mother's version of Jesus's beatitude, "Everything is good when you're hungry," taught us to recognize everything as good, even our hunger.

10

And you just came from church!

Mom was a devout Catholic. That meant going to church – a lot. She not only went to church every Sunday but on the weekdays as well. When my brother was an altar server, she would drag me out of bed and into the car for the early bird Mass at 7:00 a.m. I remember thinking, God isn't even awake, so why are we? My brother and I went to church at least in body, although not necessarily in mind or heart. Shortly after we left church, we would start fighting. My mother would angrily vent, "And you just came from church!" I didn't get it. I didn't understand the connection between what happened inside church and what happened outside church. Mom was reminding us that what happens inside the church – the act of worship – should change us. When we walk out of church or temple or mosque or synagogue, we should be different from when we went in. She was teaching us that faith should fill us up with love and joy and hope, so much so that when we walk out we are so filled up that we overflow with happiness. She was also giving voice to the critics who question the role of religion in contemporary society. Religion preaches peace but the world remains at war. Congregations talk about love yet there are too many acts of hate. Religious doctrines proclaim social justice, but society is rife with injustice. So what difference does religion make?

A colleague helped me to gain insight into this question. I used to produce the travel show at CNN, which was hosted by one of the network's meteorologists. I remember asking her how meteorologists forecast the weather. She talked to me about something called synoptic meteorology, a method of forecasting large-scale weather systems, which uses sophisticated satellite imagery, intricate weather plots, complex prognostic charts, and elaborate computer programs to determine things like pressure tendencies, precipitation, air masses, sky cover, and wind speed. But she cautioned that any good meteorologist will always remember the last and perhaps most important method of forecasting, "Don't forget to look out the window."

I think of this example whenever I think of the connection between faith and life. Denominations make a point of having elaborate liturgies, opulent buildings, lavish rituals, luscious symbols, and beautiful music. But if no one is looking out the window to connect to what is happening in the world, what's the point?

Sadly, I think many people are like my brother and I were – worshiping in body, but not necessarily with mind or heart, safe and content in our holy huddle, unaware that there is any connection between what happens inside and outside houses of worship. Perhaps this is why our Jewish ancestors wrote in the Talmud,

"Never pray in a room without windows."

The last words we hear in the Mass are, "The Mass is ended." These words, translated from the Latin, literally mean "Go, you are sent!" That is, you have heard God's words of love, you have remembered God's justice, you have experienced God's peace. Now, go and do likewise!

The word *synoptic* means more than just a way to forecast the weather. It means to view together or to view at a common point. Faith unites believers so that they might view the world together through the eyes of love and compassion. If we took our worship to heart, then the world would proclaim with delight, "Ah, you just came from church!"

11

God help everybody

The town where we grew up, New Castle, is known as the "fireworks capital of America" because of the prominence of two local companies – Pyrotecnico: Vitale Family Fireworks and Zambelli Fireworks. The town is also known as the "hot dog capital of the world" because of its famous chili dogs. In the early 1900s, New Castle was one of the fastest growing cities in the country. Its tin plate industry attracted immigrants from around the world to work in the mills. The population of New Castle peaked in the 1950s to nearly 50,000. But after the decline of the steel industry the numbers dwindled to less than half of that. In a small town, living can be provincial. People who live in small towns are often more concerned with the happenings in their own backyard and less concerned with the news that exists beyond the town's borders, but my mom was an exception.

The first thing my mother would do when she woke up in the morning was to turn on the radio to hear the latest news, and the last thing she would do before she went to bed every night was to watch the late news on television. In between, she read the local newspaper. She was adamant about knowing what was going on not only locally but also in the world. Her awareness of the people and the places in the news helped her to relate to them in an intimate way. Mom had a nose for news and a heart directed toward the divine, so that whenever she would hear of someone suffering from poverty, pain, or loss, she would mutter, "God help everybody."

"God help everybody" might sound trite but it speaks volumes. It says that God doesn't play favorites. That alone can be scandalous to some, but Mom didn't care. "God help everybody" demonstrated the empathy she sensed with the whole human family. Mom felt that if one person was hurting, we were all somehow affected. Mom literally acted as if everyone was related. No matter where we would travel, whether to another city, state or country, she would meet people who had the same last name as someone she knew from home. She would immediately tell them about the person from home as if they were related. It was humorous, to say the least, to watch her try to connect the dots around the globe. And it was inspiring to watch her connect to the hurting people she was praying for. In one of the ladies' organizations to which Mom belonged, she helped lead the way to support the building of water towers in Africa so that the local people there could have enough clean water to drink. She gave count-less volunteer hours to help support the local hospice. And every month, she gave what she could to certain causes, especially missionaries and charities funding the poor. It was only ten dollars here and ten dollars there, but somehow that was enough to solidify the solidarity Mom felt with those most in need. "God help everybody" from New Castle, Pennsylvania, to New Castle, England, and beyond.

12

Nobody out there is any better than you

As students in elementary and middle school, my brother and I participated in several speech contests. We were prepared for competition by a nun named Sr. Jeanette. Sr. Jeanette appeared to have as much passion for coaching her students as she did for Jesus. She worked with us many a night after school. She spent most of the time on delivery, word accents, intonation, inflection, and modulation. What she didn't address, though, was performance anxiety, something that I painfully suffered. When the day of competition came, I was so nervous that I became nauseous, butterflies dancing around my abdomen as if it were a trampoline. Public speaking is still considered the number one fear for a majority of people. I was in good company, but that wasn't good enough. My brain was tainted with negative thoughts: "What if I forget a word or a whole sentence?" "What if my delivery is not what they had hoped?" "What if I have a wardrobe malfunction in the middle of the speech?" "What if I'm not good enough?" "What if they don't like me?" "What happens if I don't win?" "What if I fail miserably?" Whenever I shared my fears with my mother, she would say, "Just remember, nobody out there is any better than you." While I appreciated her affirmation and encouragement, I didn't understand what she was talking about. Of course there were people out there better than me. There were students who had been competing a lot longer than me. There were peers who looked sharper, sounded more eloquent and appeared more confident. And there were the judges who spent a majority of their professional career critiquing student contestants like us. Perhaps, but Mom was pointing me toward a reality deeper than being able to win a speech contest.

If it's true that nobody out there is any better than me, then the reverse must also be true – *I* am no better than anybody out there and winning or losing wasn't going to change that. Mom was saying that winning doesn't make us any better than anyone else, nor does losing make us inferior to anyone else. She was trying to emphasize that beyond our talents lay the reality that we are all human. She was right. All of us are born and we all die. We sleep. We wake up. We put on one sock at a time. And we are all afraid. And we all have hopes and dreams for health, happiness, prosperity, peace.

My mother was trying to tell me that we are more alike than we care to believe. Forgetting that sets up distinctions that often create barriers and generate fear. Forgetting that creates a world of me versus you and us versus them. It allows my ego to bask in the glory of victory or to be crushed in face of defeat. It means I have to prove something to be worth something. That's a lot of pressure! No wonder I was nervous.

On the other hand, remembering our common humanity ushers in a sense of calm and comfort. It says we are all in this together. It says that winning or losing doesn't prove I'm any better or worse than you. This kind of thinking drives the ego away. It tells us our self-worth isn't tied to winning or to what we can do. It gives us the freedom to be vulnerable. It enables us to revel in our God-given talents for the sake of pure joy. This frees us to make mistakes, even to fail miserably. And, typically, as I have discovered, when we allow ourselves the freedom to fail, we usually succeed. Now, that's a winning attitude!

13

Stand up straight

Sometimes in life, we don't always get what we want, but we usually get what we need. I always wanted to be tall. Tall people have a commanding presence. They don't get lost in the crowd. People are always looking up to them. I used to pray that I would grow at least a few more inches. Alas, I am short – 5′ 1″ – something I inherited from my mother. She sometimes used my smallness to her advantage – passing me off as a child to get cheaper rates – up until I was about 15 years old! That may have helped our budget but it didn't do much for my self-esteem.

Mom was about an inch or two taller than me. Though she rarely formally exercised, she was consistently rolling her shoulders back. This, she felt, helped her posture by reminding herself to stand up straight. Mom was constantly reminding us to do the same. "Stand up straight" she would say and then she would roll her shoulders back as a way of telling us that she, too, was committed to having good posture.

There is no doubt that standing up straight offers a myriad of health benefits, which is why it is one of the most common instructions mothers give to their children. But I believe our mother was pointing toward something more than just physical fitness.

When Mom said "stand up straight," she was really encouraging us to "stand tall." To her, standing tall meant being proud, being brave, and being confident, whereas slouching signified shame, weakness, and insecurity.

When I think of people who stand tall, I envision prophets and dreamers who dare to imagine a better situation against a backdrop of hopelessness; heroes who risk their lives in order to liberate the lives of others; heralds who speak out for the sake of justice no matter the cost; individuals who rise above the din of the crowd to sing their own song; people who have been to hell and back and radiate inner peace.

I think, too, of the simple ways in which my mother stood tall. Dressing properly was one of them. She always dressed to the nines and encouraged us to do the same. She frowned on my brother's wearing jeans to school. One time she made him change his shirt. He had worn it so often that there were holes in the underarms. Despite our poverty she wanted us to stand tall among our peers.

Another way in which my mother stood tall was to be on time. To my mother, integrity meant never being late. One time when Mom was visiting my brother in Florida, they were running a few minutes late for Mass. Mom made my brother turn around and drive home. She said, "We'll go to the next Mass, I hate walking in late." So, they drove home and then came back for the next Mass – on time. Being on time commands the kind of respect that is given to those who stand tall.

Our mother was only 5′ 2″, but to us she stood ten feet tall. Mom taught me that I didn't need more inches – I just needed a mother who showed me how to stand tall.

14

*Hell is full of
people like that!*

Mom was a good driver. Whether she drove our 1958 Ford Custom 300 or our 1984 Pontiac, she rarely went over the speed limit. She obeyed traffic laws even when no one was around to notice otherwise. She was attentive and alert. If she were alive today, she would never think about texting, reading, or sending an e-mail while driving. She was considerate and highly critical of those who weren't. Every time a driver would cut her off, or not allow her into a lane, or run a red light or a stop sign, or fly past us with a speed reserved for the race track, she would say, "Hell is full of people like that." I wasn't quite sure what she meant. How did she know who was in hell? As far as I knew, no one who had gone to hell came back to talk about it. On the other hand, I thought, there must be a reason why the words *speed* and *demon* are often used together, and why someone who is driving at an excessive speed is seen as moving like a "bat out of hell." Maybe Mom was on to something.

It is estimated that about a third of all traffic accidents are caused by speeding drivers. Why do we speed? We speed because we are in a hurry. We are in a hurry because we are running late. We are running late because most often we don't allow ourselves enough time to get from point A to point B. We don't allow ourselves enough time to get where we need to go because we make choices that push our time limits. Our lack of time management usually results in a lack of courtesy towards others, especially other drivers. We curse those going below the speed limit. We take chances, running red lights and stop signs, putting ourselves and others at risk. We cut people off or we don't allow them to merge in front of us. And God forbid if the driver in front of us doesn't put his foot on the accelerator the second the light turns green! When we act this way, we are behaving as though our needs are more important than anyone else's. We are saying, "I don't care if you need to get somewhere, because I am late to my appointment."

When my mother said, "Hell is full of people like that," she was speaking of people who only think of themselves, who continually put their lives and their needs before the lives and needs of others. Heaven, then, must be full of people who behave in the opposite way; people who put the needs of others before their own. Mom demonstrated this over and over again, especially while driving. I remember riding in the front seat of the car before the days of seat belts. When we would have to make a sudden stop, Mom would instinctively move her right arm over my chest to protect me from hitting the windshield. That simple gesture spoke volumes.

By shielding me, she left herself open to harm, indicating her willingness to put someone else's life ahead of her own. It was an act of love that contained a glimpse of heaven. If we all adopted more of an attitude of concern for others, we would have a bit more heaven on earth, or at least, on the highways.

15

My brother and I didn't need news reports about corporate corruption to teach us that lying was wrong. We had Violet. When my mother said, "Don't lie," it came from deep in the resonance of her chest with undertones of retribution as if she knew we already had. Mom detested lying and she had no use for liars.

It was pointless to lie to my mother. She would eventually figure out the truth, if she didn't already know it. Her attitude helped me to see how grievous lying can be, especially the lies we tell ourselves.

On certain Mondays, Mom and I would leave early in the morning to drive to Pittsburgh for "clinic Mondays." Clinic gave the professional team, everyone from plastic and oral-maxillofacial specialists to speech therapists and social workers, the chance to discuss with one another the needs of each patient. And it gave us patients the opportunity to see all of our care specialists in one appointment. I hated those Mondays. It was painful to see other children who were also born with cleft lips and palates. I fooled myself into thinking that I was different, that I didn't look like them, that I wasn't broken like they were. The truth was, I was no different, I did look like them, and I was just as broken as they were.

Sometimes the truth hurts. Sometimes it's brutally painful. That's why we fear the truth, and that's why we avoid those who confront us with it. Lying gives us a temporary escape. It tricks us into thinking we can avoid the pain of the truth. So we hide behind things like obsessions, compulsions, addictions, dependencies, and codependencies rather than face the truth. For me, it was easier to hide behind the need to please people so they would accept me rather than to face my own brokenness. Mom, too, was forced to face her own painful truth. Her husband died after just seven years of marriage, leaving her widowed with two young children. Instead of running away from the truth, she embraced it by being the best mom she could be. "Don't lie" was her way of teaching us that avoiding the pain of the truth only perpetuates it; that the more we try to elude the truth, the more it pursues us; that it is, in the end, much easier to accept the pain of reality than to live a lie. As the gospel tells us and as my mother knew, "the truth will set you free" – free to be true to yourself, free to live a life without fear, free to live a life born of authenticity, which freely sees the truth, freely hears the truth, and freely speaks the truth.

16

How many times have I told you? "Keep your mouth shut"

Thanks to Mom, I discovered at an early age the part of our bodies that gets us into trouble the most: the tongue! Whenever she asserted, "How many times have I told you, 'Keep your mouth shut,'" I knew I had spilled something she wanted kept quiet. The fact that she said this to me often told me that I had a hard time controlling my tongue. Sometimes I still do. But at least now I know why. As a singer who has studied the anatomy of the voice, I learned that the tongue is the strongest muscle in the body. If left to its own will, it will take control. For the singer, that means wreaking havoc by causing tension in the voice. Ironically, singers produce the most beautiful, free-sounding notes not by engaging the tongue, but by getting it out of the way. They spend years training and practicing different techniques in order to learn how to do this. Mom's method for getting the tongue out of the way was much simpler: "Keep your mouth shut."

Out of all of Mom's sayings, this may be the one that continues to haunt me the most. There are so many times when soon after words have slipped off my tongue, through my lips, and into the cosmos, I've wished I could just reach out to pull them back in. It is so easy to spit out words, but oh so hard to take them back – just ask any politician or celebrity who has made a discriminatory remark. And, with the invention of the Internet, it is virtually impossible to get the words back. Once thrust into cyberspace, our words are sure to live on long after we do, which reminds me of a similar axiom of Mom's.

Almost as often as she used to say, "Keep your mouth shut," Mom would caution, "Think before you say something." My mother was trying to remind us that before we open our mouth, we need a good dose of mindfulness. Mindfulness helps us to be aware of what it is we are about to say. It causes us to stop and consider whether what we have to say is positive and virtuous or poisonous trash talk, whether our speech is worth listening to, or whether we are simply rambling because we like to hear ourselves talk.

We've all encountered persons who talk a lot but ultimately say nothing, whereas the wisest among us seem to be people of very few words. These are the persons who have discovered that it is more important to listen to others than to hear the sound of their own voice. They personify the underlying reality of my mother's adage, which is that we simply talk too much and listen too little. That's because the ego, like the tongue, loves to be in control. The ego tells me that what I have to say is more important than what you have to say. The ego is uncomfortable with silence. The ego claims that if I am silent, I don't matter. Strangely enough, the times in our lives that matter the most are usually times of absolute silence, times for which there are no words: the loss of a loved one, the birth of a child, a terminal diagnosis, or an unexpected miracle. Mom knew about these times. She experienced them aplenty. She understood that God speaks mostly in the silence, in between the words. In saying "Keep your mouth shut," she was echoing one of my favorite mottoes from Mozart, "The music is not in the notes, but in the silence between."

17

C'mon, get up, there's work to be done

I never needed an alarm clock to wake me up. Mom's morning ritual took care of that. Every morning at 6:00 a.m. Mom would either put away the pots and pans from dinner the night before or begin cooking for the day ahead. In any case, the clanging and banging was so loud, I wondered if my mom was engaged in a secret competition with the rooster down the street to see who could be the first to wake up the neighborhood. Many of my friends slept until noon during the summer and on the weekends, but that would have been unthinkable in my house. If John wasn't yet awake, Mom would go into his room in the early morning and open the curtains to let the sun in. As daylight burst its rays onto

John's face, Mom would say, "C'mon, get up, there's work to be done."

Mom wasn't one to rest. She was up at 6:00 a.m. every day – even on weekends – even on vacation. With two children, a house, a dog, and a yard to take care of, there was much that needed to be done. For Mom, work was a prime motivator. She didn't have to punch a clock. She didn't have a boss. She didn't have to report to anyone. It was the work itself that prompted her to get out of bed in the morning. Sometimes I think work is what kept her going. Work gave her a focus and much more.

Mom wasn't a career woman. She didn't go to college. She didn't have a high-paying job. She never got a promotion. She never got a raise or a bonus check. But to us, Mom demonstrated the value of an honest day's work. Her labor was born out of necessity. Her work included tasks ranging from hanging the laundry to taking her children to swimming lessons. That she found joy in her daily chores was obvious. She did every task with great care and it showed. She ironed our bed sheets and pillowcases as if they were going to be packaged for sale at Bloomingdale's. They were so perfectly pleated and folded, I hated to unfold them! She scrubbed the kitchen as if Mr. Clean were coming for dinner. She meticulously swept the floor until every last atom of dust was gone. Then, she mopped the floor – even the baseboards got a bath – and then thoroughly and thoughtfully waxed it on her hands and knees – every nook and cranny included. We weren't allowed to set foot on that floor until it was completely dry.

By doing her work with such attentiveness, she brought significance to the simplest of tasks. She proved that all work can bring meaning and purpose to our lives – whether it's finding a cure for cancer or drying the dishes. She taught us how work boosts our self-esteem. There is an inner feeling of gratification that comes from honest toil. When we look back at the work we have done, there is a healthy sense of accomplishment, especially when we can see the fruits of our labor. The fruits of my mother's labor, her children, are living testimonies to the dignity and integrity of my mother's work.

"C'mon, get up there's work to be done" told us that there was something awaiting us each day that required our gifts. By summoning us to rise from our sleep, Mom was telling us that our efforts were needed. In calling us out of bed this way, she established a sense of hopeful anticipation for the day ahead. My mother's saying commissioned her children to share in her work, much like Jesus did when he commissioned his disciples by saying, "The harvest is rich, but the workers are few."

18

The time nobody sees, but the work everybody sees

I grew up in a house on a little over five acres. Where our property ended, a dairy farm began. Most of our land was not developed. But Mom saw to it that the part that was ours was kept perfectly pristine. Every so often, Mom would don an off-white sleeveless button-down cotton shirt stained with spots of paint, brown polyester pants with elastic at the top, a gold chiffon scarf and a baseball cap to cover her head, and garden gloves. When she dressed this way, we knew where she was headed – out to edge our driveway. Her tools: an ax, two stakes, string, and a pillow. We had a limestone driveway. The grass, weeds, and other migrant brush tried to encroach on the driveway and Mom would have none of that. It was Mom against the weeds. My mother would kneel on a pillow to protect her knees. She would drive a stake into the ground and tie a piece of string to it. Next, she would tie the other end of the string to another stake and drive it into the ground. The string helped her to keep the edge straight. Then, she would use her ax to painstakingly clear away, one by one, any and all of the weeds that were destroying the line of a flawless edge. Because our driveway was about 75 feet long, it would take her hours, even days to complete the job. But she didn't care. She didn't mind that it took a long time, or that the sun and heat made her face as red as a beet, or that her shoulder hurt from the constant motion of throwing down the ax, or that her back hurt from strain. All she cared about was how it looked when she was finished.

Mom never cared for short cuts. She knew that everything worthwhile takes time. She took time with everything she did, whether it was cooking, baking, cleaning, ironing, organizing an event for one of her ladies' organizations, or

The time nobody sees, but the work...

running the Italian pastry booth at the church bazaar. I, on the other hand, was the opposite. I liked to get things done fast so that I could cross them off my list and move on to the next project. My goal was productivity; Mom's was precision. Both are worthy goals and my mother was trying to teach me how to strike a balance between the two.

Mom's version of the familiar axiom "Haste makes waste" was "The time nobody sees, but the work everybody sees." She would say this to me every time I rushed to complete something. If Mom was the head of a manufacturing corporation she would probably have "The time nobody sees, but the work everybody sees" engraved on plaques over every work station. Her wisdom taught me that when we do things in a hurry, we make mistakes. Then we end up redoing what we did, spending twice as much time as we would have spent if we had taken the time required in the first place. When we are so driven toward production, we forget about the importance of process. Companies who have experienced a recall or a manufacturing disaster learn this the hard way. When human error is to blame, it is usually because someone chose to put productivity ahead of precision. Someone chose to cut corners. My mother's saying reminds me of the chaos that can ensue when we cut corners. Luckily for us, Mom didn't cut corners. The edges of our driveway said it all.

19

Learn how to do things

My mother was married only seven years when her husband died. In those days, widows didn't remarry and if they did, they waited a long time. Our mother never married again. So my brother John became the "man of the house," a responsibility he took seriously – a responsibility that led him to be overzealous at times.

John was always trying to build or fix something. He would see a project or plan in a book or magazine and think, "I can make that." But he would dive into things without really knowing what he was doing. He used our father's tools without really understanding their function. For example, we had a large table saw in the cellar that was kept shrouded by a blue blanket. I was sure there was a person who lived underneath, but I was too afraid to find out. The saw we had at the time used a blade best suited for cross cutting (across the grain) as opposed to vice rip cutting (with the grain), so when my brother tried rip cutting with it, the motor began to smoke. It's a wonder he didn't cut a finger off.

On another occasion he tried to replace the fuel filter in our car. Replacing the fuel filter begins by detaching the fuel line from the carburetor, which involves loosening a fitting that connects the two together. Normally, the fitting rotates freely around the fuel line, but when my brother tried to change the filter, the fitting was stuck. He tried to force it to turn and ended up putting a hole in the fuel line. To say that Mom was not happy would be a gross understatement! I can still hear her response echoing throughout the universe. It was in these contexts that my mom would say, "Learn how to do things."

Mom wanted us to "learn how to do things" so we would do them the right way. She was trying to teach us the importance of doing our homework, of adequate preparation. We only needed to observe her baking processes to understand what she was trying to develop in us.

My mother's kitchen was her kingdom and in it she reigned supreme. Mom was an artist and the kitchen was her canvas. Like many artists, she practiced her art for many, many years until it became as much a part of her as her right hand. Like most great bakers, she learned from other great bakers – her mother, for one. Everything she prepared, especially her cookies, was unequaled. While she had the ability to bake many cookies, she concentrated on the three she knew best: Italian pizzelles, wedding cookies and Polish kruschiki's. She made these cookies so often, she didn't need a recipe. Every once in a while she would allow us to help, but our efforts paled in comparison to the master baker. To Mom, *every* detail mattered. She was a perfectionist who demanded the same from her children. As she coached us how to roll a piece of dough into a seamless ball to make a wedding cookie, she showed us what it meant to hone a craft. She taught us that it takes years and years of practice to become a true artist, to "learn how to do things." She showed us that true artists never stop learning and growing in their craft.

We live in an age of instant gratification – where results are far more important than processes. If you want a recipe, "Google it." If you want to make or build something, you will likely find some sort of instructional video on YouTube. But this can never compare to watching and/or learning from a master craftsman or chef. To me, there is nothing more inspiring than experiencing the gifts of a true artist firsthand. Witnessing the passion, single-mindedness, care, and concentration with which an artist works is beyond compare. In our house, we had all of that and more. We literally got to sink our teeth into our mother's art – tasting the sweetness of Mom's knowledge.

20

Just taste it

Mom wasn't the kind of parent who told my brother and me that we had to eat our vegetables. Nor did she threaten us with going to bed without dessert if we didn't eat what she served. And when it came to food, I was the queen of picky. I wouldn't eat cheese, condiments, lunch meats or anything creamy or white, which cut out most casseroles and anything made with mayonnaise. Chicken salad? No way! Green bean casserole? Not me! To be honest, I had never even tried a lot of these foods. But by their looks and their smell, I just automatically anticipated that I wouldn't like them, so I was afraid to try them. Whenever I would turn my nose up at something, my mother would simply say, "Just taste it!" What she didn't say was, "You have to eat this." Nor did she say, "You have to like this." In saying "Just taste it," she allowed me a great deal of freedom. That freedom gave me the reassurance I needed to take the first forkful.

Mom invited us to try new things all the time. When my brother John was in the 9th grade, Mom suggested he take a summer course at the local vocational technical school. He wasn't crazy about the idea, but he signed up for a six-week course in auto mechanics. He liked it so much, he signed up for a course the following summer – this time, in bricklaying.

Throughout my life, I have observed the bounty of what can happen when people "Just taste it." I began work at CNN eight years after the network launched. The early years were challenging to say the least. People scoffed at Ted Turner's vision for a 24-hour news network. Instead of calling it Cable News Network, cynics called it "Chicken Noodle News." Ted's attitude was, "Just taste it." Well, "Chicken Noodle News" tasted good enough to millions of viewers who continue to feast on its 24-hour news menu, not to mention the networks that copied its format.

Those magic words, "Just taste it," come back to me whenever I'm afraid to try something new. I remind myself, "I don't have to love this," or, "I don't have to do this all my life." Now I know how to give myself the freedom I need to try new things. That has meant trying ice skating and in-line skating in my 30s, learning tap and ballroom dancing and playing mah-jongg in my 40s, and learning how to play the cello at 50. Trying new things helps get us out of our box. It moves us beyond ourselves to encounter a different experience. New foods, new clothes, new styles, new books, new works of art, new modes of entertainment, new relationships – all keep life fresh, inventive, energized. Go ahead, "Just taste it." But beware. You just might like it.

21

Eat slow and
chew your food

My mother's mother knew what it was like to live off the land. She grew up in the tiny Italian village of San Bartolomeo in Galdo in the region of Campania, about 75 miles northeast of Naples. Her family ate the plants and animals they farmed. Grandma would tell stories of how she would catch, kill, and then cook the chickens that came from her back yard. She knew what organic meant long before it was fashionable. When she came to the United States and settled in western Pennsylvania, farming was limited, but she still managed to maintain a vegetable garden with plenty of tomatoes to can. We would reap the benefits, eating fresh tomato sauce all year long. For Grandma, food was the heart of the matter. She knew that communities that take the time to plant, raise, cultivate, and reap their own food also take their time to eat and enjoy it. When you're Italian, you don't get away with gulping down food. Multicourse meals spread over several hours are part of everyday life. It's no wonder that cultures like these seem more rooted, more bonded, more vibrant. The people who dwell in these lands understand the power of food to create and to sustain relationships. That's why they tend to have at least one meal a day that is eaten very s-l-o-w-l-y.

Our holiday meals were the epitome of eating slowly. They were seven-course feasts that began around 2:00 in the afternoon and ended around 4:00 or 5:00 with conversations lingering into the evening. Those meals served to cement our extended family together. While we didn't eat this way every day, we did manage to eat together every night. That's when Mom would say, "Eat slow and chew your food." She wasn't just saying that to aid our digestive system, she was doing her part to strengthen family ties. She was reminding us that food, like life, was meant to be savored, not simply consumed.

Today, we have come to know life in the fast lane, where drive-thru fast food has become the norm instead of the exception. We act as though food is an interruption in our day, something that we have to do in order to make it through the day, rather than an experience to relish. What could be more important than nourishment? Our fast food frenzy has led to unhealthy eating habits and unhealthy lifestyles. In order to counteract the fast food lifestyle, a Slow Food movement was born in the 1980s. Where else? In Italy! The Slow Food movement, which now exists in 150 countries, promotes conviviality over convenience by preserving the practice of local food production. The aim of this movement is to help people become more attentive to the food they eat, more aware of where it comes from, and more grateful for every bite. As Mom knew, this happens more often when we "eat slowly and chew our food." We need to eat to live, but Mom, like her mother, encouraged us to live to eat, by savoring every morsel that touched our palate.

22 *Everything in moderation*

Like many people, Mom was always on a diet. She would take a break from dieting to splurge during the holidays. But before she went to bed, she would enthusiastically announce, "Tomorrow, I start my diet!" My brother also loved to eat (he still does). My brother and I would have contests when we were young. He would try to lose weight and I would try to gain weight. We would compete to see who could lose or gain more pounds in the shortest amount of time.

When Mom wanted to lose a few pounds, she became a member of the TOPS club; that's the acronym for Take Off Pounds Sensibly. According to TOPS, all foods can fit into a diet, *in moderation*. But even before Mom joined the willful women of TOPS, she would repeatedly

AS MAMA USED TO SAY

remind us, "Everything in moderation."

One night, my brother, hungry for dessert, stuck his head in the refrigerator and found what he was looking for – a huge piece of lemon icebox cake. Lemon ice box cake, as our mother made it, is a dessert layered with lemon pudding, angel food cake, and whipped cream. He took the whole thing and grabbed a fork. Mom, standing nearby, couldn't resist. "Are you going to eat all that?" she asked. My brother said, "Yes." Then Mom said in Italian dialect, "Con moderazione, esso durerà." My brother said, "What does that mean?" And, Mom said "In moderation, it will endure." She went on in English, "If you eat all that cake today, when you come back to the refrigerator tomorrow, there will be none left. If you only eat half of it now, then when you come back tomorrow, the other half will be left to eat." My brother thought about it. He really wanted the whole thing. He mustered up his willpower and decided to cut the piece of cake in half. Sure enough, the next day came and the other half of the cake was there waiting to be eaten.

Mom didn't only preach moderation in our diets. She also applied it to other areas of life: clothing, material goods, money, activities, watching television and so on. She was advising us that too much of anything, even something good, can be harmful. It's a lesson that has continued to teach.

Covering travel stories for CNN took me around the globe. It was always interesting to witness the evolution of a new tourist site, especially sites considered to be natural or historic. When these new sites first opened, visitors would come in great numbers, often to the detriment of the site itself. Not long after the sites were opened, limits were placed on the numbers of visitors and on their activities. The regulations were meant to safeguard and protect the sites for years to come. Mom may have comprehended the consequences of carbon footprints long before it became fashionable. "Everything in moderation" has huge implications for our climate and even broader significance for our society. Her adage offers foresight into what might happen if we consume in moderation instead of greed. It teaches us the wisdom of aiming to achieve a balance in all things. It helps us to see that living in moderation might ensure a brighter future for generations to come.

23 *A little bit of consideration*

Whenever I pull into a grocery store parking lot, I'm struck by how many shopping carts are scattered all over the place. Could it be that the carts have a mind of their own? That they drive themselves all over Kroger-town to compete for shoppers' attention? More than likely after shoppers unload their paper towels, Pampers, and peas, they are just too tired or too lazy to return their cart to its corral or to the store itself. This may seem trivial, but the ramifications might be anything but. Other shoppers can't easily park because there are shopping carts in the way. A strong gust of wind might blow a cart into a car, damaging both the cart and the car. The grocery store has to repair or replace the cart, passing the expense onto the consumer by raising the price of groceries. The point is this: everything we do has an effect on someone else. Mom had a remark for these kinds of situations: "A little bit of consideration." What she meant was that a little bit of consideration goes a long way, and that one person's laziness is often another person's burden.

Though sometimes, Mom didn't practice what she preached. Often when she went to the grocery store, she used to park in the handicapped spots when there were no other convenient parking spots available. One time, during a volunteer shift at the local hospital, she parked in a space reserved for doctors only! Well, Doctor Kuczka got a taste of her own medicine when her car was stolen from that spot. Luckily for her, the police found her car the next day with her purse in it – all intact. God is good.

Mom might have parked in the wrong spots at times, but she showed consideration in so many ways: whenever there was one piece of chicken left, or one last bite of anything from dinner, she would first ask my brother and me if we wanted it – every time. She would go out in the cold to start the car in the deep of winter so that we would be warm when we got into it. Each time we got in the car, she gave up control of the radio so that I could listen to what I wanted. Each time we took a plane trip, she gladly sat in the middle so that I could have the window seat. Every operation (before the days of outpatient surgery), she arranged child care for my brother and left home in the wee hours of the morning to travel 50 miles to Pittsburgh to see me before I went into the operating room because she knew what that meant to me – every surgery. And she would show up at funeral homes and at funerals for people with whom she had a minor connection, simply to offer support and care.

Each day, life presents us with a million opportunities to show "A little bit of consideration": smiling at people, holding the door open for others, conversing with cashiers by using their names, picking up the dog poop, even if it is buried in the grass or the pine straw. All it takes, as my mother would also say is, "A little bit of effort." As my mother knew, a little bit of consideration makes a *big* difference.

24

Shut off these lights because the utility company doesn't get mad

As a child, I was afraid of the dark, so wherever I went in the house, I would leave the lights on. Whenever my mother came by and no one was in that particular room she would say, "Shut off these lights because the utility company doesn't get mad." I used to have visions of men clad in their utility company shirts and caps with big frowns on their faces whenever Mom shut off the lights. Though the cost of lighting a house is relatively inexpensive, Mom was teaching us a lesson in saving money.

Mom lived on a fixed income. After the death of our father, she lived on Social Security, which limited the amount of income she could earn from a job. Once we were both in middle school, she worked as a part-time server at our school cafeteria. She also worked at a china factory until she secured full-time employment at the county courthouse.

These days, it is sometimes difficult for a two-income family to make ends meet, so I think back with awe at how my mother was able to raise two children on her own with a meager income *and* be able to balance her checkbook. Though Grandma and Aunt Mary helped us out financially, my mother did her part to keep expenses under control. Turning off the lights and other electronic devices like the television when they weren't in use was one way we saved money. But there were others. We rarely ate out. We ate at home every night, except for an occasional fast food run. On special occasions, such as Mother's Day, we would eat out at a nice restaurant. If we took a vacation, we traveled by car or by train. Most of our summer vacations were spent on Long Island, where my mother's brother and his family lived. Uncle Harry and

Aunt Carolyn were extremely generous in allowing us to stay with them and in taking us to the hottest tourist spots on Long Island and in "the Big Apple." My mother never had a major credit card. Imagine that! She carried credit cards for retail stores such as Sears or JCPenney, but if she charged something, she always paid it off the next month. If she saw something we needed, she would often put it on layaway. Most of the time, if she didn't have the money, she didn't buy it. If all of us lived like that, including societies and governments, it would be a different world!

Mom was the queen of the "Do-it-yourself" method! My dad built our house but Mom was the one who maintained it. She cleaned the house, inside and out. She mowed the lawn and then raked and bagged the clippings. In the spring, she replaced the storm windows with screens and reversed the process in the winter. Every so often, she would paint the basement – the whole basement, walls, floors, steps – you name it. She was focused on and committed to the upkeep of the house and the yard.

Mom's penchant for DIY rubbed off on her children. When my brother John was in high school, he worked at Henry's Auto Body Shop and bought his first car, a 1967 Ford Mustang, from Henry for $150.00. The car had belonged to Henry's son and had been in a wreck, so it needed some repair. My brother bought the parts needed – a fender, hood, and front valence panel – at a junkyard for a few hundred dollars. Because John worked at an auto body repair shop, he was able to repair the car himself. To John, the process of buying and fixing a damaged car was worth far more than having the money to purchase a better one.

Though we didn't have a lot of money, we never wanted for anything. By saying, "Shut off these lights because the utility company doesn't get mad," Mom was shedding light on saving money by teaching us that counting pennies now might bring about a financial future we could count on.

25

*I'm sending a letter
to Ralph Nader!*

I grew up in the 1960s and 70s, decades marked by protests for civil rights, for and against U.S. involvement in the Vietnam War, and for individual freedoms. During that time, Mom had her own kind of protests. Whenever she felt her rights as a consumer were being violated, she fought back with this message, "I'm sending a letter to Ralph Nader!"

Ralph Nader, a lawyer, political aide, and consumer advocate hit the headlines in the mid-60s by writing a book called *Unsafe at Any Speed*, which criticized the safety standards of U.S. automobiles. Nader's advocacy helped to pass the 1966 National Traffic and Motor Vehicle Safety Act, which mandated safety features in automobiles, including seat belts. Nader inspired activists, known as "Nader's raiders," to help him bring about justice for consumers.

For some reason, Mom seemed to connect with Mr. Nader. No matter what issue she had with a product, she would continually threaten the company who made it by saying "I'm sending a letter to Ralph Nader!" I don't know if she ever sent a letter to Mr. Nader and if she did, I'm not sure that he wrote back. Her point was to get an answer and she used Nader's name as if he were the consumer god who would have been glad to wave his magic wand for Vi Kuczka. She became an unofficial member of Nader's raiders.

Some years after Nader's book was published, Mom bought a 1969 Chevrolet Caprice. That car included a new feature – a thermostat that allowed the driver to set the inside temperature of the car, something that is now standard in many cars. Unfortunately, ours never worked. Mom called the dealership to complain. She wasn't satisfied with the answers she was given.

I'm sending a letter to Ralph Nader!

She persisted with her protest until she reached the top management, writing a letter to the CEO of General Motors. Unfortunately, nothing was ever resolved. But in that instance, my mother showed us what it meant to be a consumer advocate.

We would hear Mom on the phone when she was challenging companies for not living up to the promise of their products. She always, *always* asked for the person's name – whether it was the operator, the receptionist, or the vice president. She would typically ask to speak to the manager. Once she had the manager on the phone, he had no chance. She wouldn't take no for an answer. She wouldn't let the conversation end until she received some type of satisfaction, even if it meant the satisfaction of having the last word by saying "I'm sending a letter to Ralph Nader!" Mom would write to the leaders of companies, stating her case, threatening to never buy their products again – reinforcing another one of her favorite sayings, "Money talks."

My mom, a poor widow, stood up to several multi-billion-dollar companies. In her poverty, she challenged the powerful. She reminded me of the parable of the widow who hounded the corrupt judge so much that he eventually granted her request. She hounded heads of corporations with the persistence of a prophet. Mom taught us the only way to right wrongdoing is to speak up and to speak out – especially to those who have the power to affect change. She gifted us with invaluable lessons: to not be afraid to contact someone by phone, even CEOs; to stand up for our rights; and to be persistent in our follow-up. My mother, like her mentor Ralph Nader, showed us the difference that can be made by one person.

26

*The harder I try,
the worse it is*

Like most writers, I know what it means to experience writer's block. Writer's block feels like
my brain has decided to vacate in a desert that
is devoid of words. I sit in front of a blank page
for hours awaiting inspiration that doesn't come.
Agonized and frustrated, I wrinkle my brow,
thinking that will somehow propel my creative
juices into action. It doesn't. I try sitting at another angle to see if that will make a difference.
It doesn't. I call out to the saints who were great
writers: Ephrem the Syrian, Hildegard of Bingen,
and St. Anthony, patron saint of finding things,
for help in finding words. No matter how hard
I try, nothing happens. It reminds me of when
my mother used to say, "The harder I try, the
worse it is."

My mother wasn't a writer, but she knew what it felt like to try to do something in vain.

In saying "The harder I try, the worse it is," Mom was expressing frustration. But she was also trying to teach us about the wisdom of letting go.

Like Mom, we all want to see the results of our labor. We want to know that our efforts are paying off. When we come up empty over and over, we have two choices: we can either try harder or simply let go. Most of us choose to try harder because we are not willing to accept defeat. Defeat is a blow to our ego. It signals failure, something most of us find hard to swallow. Trying harder masks our ego's fear of self-doubt. Trying harder tells us that we are the solution. It fools us into thinking that we are ultimately in control, that our fate is in our hands.

Letting go, on the other hand, helps us to accept what is, even if that means defeat. Letting go carries the risk of being vulnerable, because it acknowledges our weakness. It allows us to recognize that our destiny is often out of our hands. It tells us that we might be part of the problem, rather than the solution. It prompts us to get out of the way, allowing our situation to unfold naturally. Letting go transforms our fears into trust.

St. Hildegard said, "Trust shows the way." When we let go and trust, things happen. I don't know if Hildegard ever experienced writer's block. But if she did, she probably would have shared my anxiety, my doubt, and my unease. My mother's words of frustration, "The harder I try, the worse it is," moves me to walk away from my computer, do something else, and forget about trying to write. Strangely enough, when I do this, the words come.

27

Death disrupts everything

Mom experienced a lot of those deaths – perhaps more than her fair share. Her father died in 1953 when she was 25. Her husband died in 1967, followed by her brother Victor in 1970 and her brother Harry in 1974. No matter who passed away, family or friend, Mom would remark, "Death disrupts everything."

Mom knew the disruptive nature of death. So did my brother and me. We experienced death's disarray with the passing of our father when John was six and I was four. Though we were very young, we saw how death interrupted life. Death was like a thief who came into the house in the middle of the night, rummaged through every drawer, and tossed all order into disorder. Nothing was ever the same after the death of our father. That's what death does. It changes life as we know it.

Most religions believe that there is some kind of life after death. Christianity was founded on this precept. Life on earth is seen as only a brief period of time, while life after death is acclaimed as eternal. But during our life on earth, there are a lot of little deaths that take place: the broken relationships and the betrayals, the trials and the tribulations, the disappointments and the despair. These little deaths mimic our final death because each of them has the potential to bring about new life. Mom's most profound experience of one of these "little deaths" occurred several years before she passed away.

In December of 1992, Mom suffered a severe cerebral hemorrhage and was taken by helicopter to a hospital in Pittsburgh. My brother was living in Goldsboro, North Carolina, at the time, and I was living in Atlanta. We headed home only to find Mom lying motionless in the neuro-intensive care unit. While she could open her eyes, she showed no signs that she was aware of who we were, where she was, or what had taken place. We waited by her bedside to see if she would talk, move – anything. The hours seemed like days. The days seemed like months. After a week, the doctor decided to operate. It was New Year's Eve. After the surgery, the doctor told us, "If she utters anything in the next 24 hours, even if it is gibberish, that is a good sign."

I'll never forget what happened that evening. My brother and I were hovered over Mom's hospital bed. We were saying good night to her and getting ready to leave when she started to talk. My brother and I looked at each other in absolute awe. She said, "I have to pee." To us, that not-so-elegant statement was like poetry! It was as if someone who was dead had come back to life. At that moment, I realized that it is much better to die and to rise than never to die at all.

The next morning, Mom was sitting up

in a chair, fully alert, when her brother walked in. "Hi Frank," she said. Again, we were astonished. Mom was back. But, the road to recovery was anything but easy. Weeks of physical and months of cognitive therapy lay ahead. During that time, my brother and I commuted back and forth from our homes to Pennsylvania. Two weeks after her surgery, I went to visit her at the hospital. She was sitting in a wheelchair. Her hair was messy and her clothes were disheveled. Here was this stoic woman who was always dressed to the nines, whose hair was always perfect, and whose makeup always looked like it was done by a professional now appearing completely vulnerable. Rarely had I seen that side of her and it was a beautiful thing to see. The doctor told us she would never be able to do more than make a slice of toast. But he didn't know Vi Kuczka. She made a miraculous recovery and was able to do almost everything she did before the stroke. But she was left with mild aphasia which kept her fragile and more charming than ever. Mom went from stoic to sensitive, from tenacious to tender. That's what death does. It "disrupts everything" so that we might be transformed into our true selves.

28 *We live from day to day*

Mom was a dancer – not a professional dancer, but give her an inch of the rug and she would cut it like nobody's business. At weddings, she would be one of the first persons out on the dance floor doing the tarantella, the chicken dance, or the polka. I remember when the troupe *Up with People* – an organization that brings young people together to travel the world and perform – came to town in 1975. Mom and I went to see them and sat close to the stage. During the last song, they came into the audience to lure people on stage to dance with them. Because we were sitting near the stage, I had a suspicion that they would look to us, so being the shy preteen that I was, I lowered my head and crouched down in my seat. Mom did the opposite. She was sitting on the edge of her seat with a look on her face that said "Pick me, pick me." And they did. She got on stage as if she were part of the act, dancing and clapping and loving every minute. At the time, I was a little embarrassed. The local paper, *The New Castle News*, covered the event and snapped a photo of the audience members on stage with the performers. The picture was in the newspaper the next day. It captured everything. There was Mom, center stage with a smile as wide as Texas. I cherish that picture now, along with the memory. It depicted the way Mom lived – fully alive in the moment.

Mom understood the importance of living every moment to the fullest. She knew all too well how life could be changed in an instant. She would often say to us, "We live from day to day." Sometimes, she would couple that with another saying, "We don't know what's going to happen from one day to the next." Both of these statements taught us the merits of living each day to the fullest – attentive to each moment.

Living in the moment is one of life's most profound experiences, and one of the most challenging. The truth is we often escape the present moment by focusing on anything but. Our mind continuously and unconsciously wanders far from the now. Perhaps we are trying to avoid the pain or boredom of the present moment, and we believe that focusing on something other than the present will bring us more pleasure than what the now has to offer. But this is an illusion. All we have is now. When we deny the present moment its due, we deny ourselves the opportunity of living life to the fullest. Mom figured this out early on.

"We live from day to day" taught us to bring mindfulness to the moment at hand. That means being present and conscious in every instant. That means instead of just going through the motions of taking a shower while our mind wanders about what the day will bring, we actually feel the water as it splashes over us, we notice the beauty and wonder of our bodies, we take pleasure in the sensation of being cleansed. Being mindful of the moment can make even the most trivial tasks – the things we typically take for granted – incredibly meaningful.

"We live from day to day" brings comfort when we are facing a crisis, a serious illness, an arduous task, or an overwhelming schedule. It reminds us that there is no need to look beyond today – that today is all we have – and that focusing on today will be enough. This is the wisdom in the Lord's Prayer – "Give us *this* day our daily bread."

"We live from day to day" also presumes that we may not be here tomorrow. It echoes a verse from Psalm 90, which speaks of the brevity of life: "Teach us to number our days aright, that we may gain gladness of heart." So live for today – seize the moment, enjoy it, and don't be afraid to get up and dance!

29

Whose fault is that?

Whenever I complained to my mother that I was tired because I had stayed up way past my bedtime the night before, or whenever I complained that I had too much homework to do on a Sunday night because I had squandered most of my weekend, or whenever the outside temperature was freezing and I complained that my hands were cold because I chose not to wear gloves, I didn't get much sympathy. Instead, Mom would respond, "Whose fault is that?" What I find interesting is that she didn't come right out and say, "That's your fault." She framed her response into a question – a question that could only be answered by me – a question whose answer revealed that I was the cause of my own dilemmas.

Answering the question "Whose fault is that?" was easy. Admitting the deeper truth – that I was the source of my own predicament – was hard. It was, after all, so much easier just to complain – especially when I could link my complaining with blaming others for my afflictions.

While some states have no-fault auto insurance and no-fault divorce, Mom didn't run a no-fault household. She knew when to call a spade a spade. Rather than look to others for the cause of my misery, "Whose fault is that?" moved me to look at myself. Mom was trying to teach me to accept responsibility for my actions, to hold myself accountable for my problems.

"Whose fault is that?" taught me that we are often the source of our own chaos, though we seldom recognize that fact because we're too busy finding fault in everyone else. Whenever I would point out somebody else's faults, Mom had another saying for me, "Worry about yourself." Instead of wondering why others are the way they are, Mom prodded me to ask myself why I am the way I am. Instead of wondering why others do the things they do, Mom prompted me to ask myself why I do the things I do. Instead of trying hopelessly to change others, Mom challenged me to change myself. Sooner or later, we all discover that the only person we can really change is ourselves.

Mom isn't here now to listen to my lamenting or to ask "Whose fault is that?" So whenever I find myself complaining, I hear her asking me, "Whose fault is that?" Time and again the question brings me back to introspection – leading to self-awareness, inner conversion, and transformation.

30

If you get sick, who's going to take care of you?

"If you get sick, who's going to take care of you?" was the quote, or rather the threat Mom would use whenever my brother and I would go out in the cold not properly dressed. I used to think to myself, "What do you mean? You will take care of me, you're my mom. That's what moms do." More than shirking her maternal responsibility, I think Mom was trying to teach us one of life's most important lessons: the art of self-care.

What is self-care? People often say to us, "Take care of yourself." But what does that really mean? I have always found it much easier to take care of others than to care for myself. Whenever someone needed something from me, the answer 99.9 percent of the time was yes.

But, all those yeses ultimately resulted in physical and emotional exhaustion, not to mention a bit of built-up resentment. I should have learned much earlier from my mother, who knew when to say no, especially to my brother and me. We didn't get everything we asked for – far from it.

I remember getting bored easily, especially on Sunday afternoons when there wasn't much to do. I used to beg my mother to go to the amusement park or someplace else that was more stimulating than being at home. Her answer was no. Sunday afternoons were her downtime, time she needed for herself and time she required in order to prepare for the week ahead. She knew how to take care of herself because she knew what she needed.

Knowing what we need is at the heart of self-care. All of us have basic needs: needs for food, water, proper sleep, healthy friendships. But oftentimes we don't care enough for ourselves to meet even these basic needs. We don't eat the right foods, we don't drink enough water, we don't get enough sleep, we don't get enough exercise, we stay in toxic relationships, and so on. In other words, we make choices for ourselves that are more harmful than whole-some. Caring for ourselves helps us develop a healthy sense of self. When we have a healthy sense of self, it is easier to make healthy choices, whether it's choosing what to have for breakfast or choosing a spouse. Caring for ourselves sends an important message to ourselves and to oth-ers: I matter and you matter!

I've learned that self-care doesn't mean that we have to abandon caring for others. In fact, often it turns out to be the opposite. When we take care of ourselves, we ultimately take care of others. Wearing proper clothing to brave the cold weather, for example, not only pre-vented my brother and me from getting sick, it also thwarted a potential burden on my mother. Self-care often leads to self-sufficiency, one of the best lessons a parent could ever teach.

31

Crying isn't going to help

My mother rarely showed emotion. She was as strong as a rock – or least that's the way she appeared on the outside. The only time I saw her cry was when she experienced the death of a loved one. I, on the other hand, was a big crybaby! In fact, a good part of my childhood was spent in tears. I cried over the reality that I was being shunned by my classmates, undergoing what seemed like endless doctor visits and surgical procedures, and spending precious childhood days in the isolation of hospital rooms. I cried because I was lonely and in pain and I didn't know what else to do. I needed my mother to cry with me, to hold me and to share the pain with me. But she didn't. Whenever she saw me cry, she would say, "Don't cry," or, more often, "Crying isn't going to help." When she said this, I could feel my tears attempting to freeze in mid-stream. I wasn't sure if she was saying this because she knew it to be true from personal experience and was trying to teach me to be strong, or because my tears triggered sadness in her own soul that she refused to acknowledge.

My mother had plenty of good reasons to cry – being separated from her one true love after only a few years of marriage and being left on her own to bring up two young children. But she rarely shed a tear. Part of this is due to the deeply held values of her generation. In those days, people didn't give in to their emotions, nor did they talk about them. They simply dealt with whatever life handed them. Their attitude embodied the first words of M. Scott Peck's famous work *The Road Less Traveled*: "Life is hard." In saying, "Crying isn't going to help," Mom was encouraging me to adopt this perspective. She wanted her children to be strong.

But that kind of stoicism didn't teach me how to deal with my pain. Crying did – or so I thought at the time. Crying helped me to acknowledge my pain. Crying validated my pain. Crying is healthy to a certain extent and it is healthier to cry than to keep all of that emotion trapped inside. But I cried so much I made myself sick. For me, crying seemed to signal my immune system to lower its defenses. Mom was right – crying was no long-term solution. Crying only added more drama than was necessary and prevented me from moving past my pain. I think Mom knew all this and this was the reason she said "Crying isn't going to help" as often as she did.

Mom didn't cry, but she prayed a lot and I assume she shared her tears with God – or at least her pain. Noted author, theologian, and Franciscan priest Richard Rohr says, "Spirituality is about what you do with your pain." He's right. Pain and suffering can lead us to a profound encounter with God. Mom found strength to deal with her pain through her relationship with God. She also knew where to go for therapy – the kitchen. Cooking and baking brought her true inner joy, so she often immersed herself in those activities. Her therapy also included surrounding herself with friends who nourished, supported, and held her up in times of doubt or fear, but she also found that focusing on others, giving to others in need, was a way to heal her own pain. And she was thankful for everything.

Although it didn't seem so at the time, I ultimately learned a lot from my mother about how to deal with pain. I, too, found strength in prayer by going to the ancient Hebrews and their psalms of lament. In lamenting my woes to God, I joined the world's oldest therapy group. Praying the psalms of lament gave me a tool stronger than tears to work through my pain – it gave me words. And while my mother turned to cooking, I turned to the performing arts as a tool for healing. Singing, acting, and dancing have brought me a great deal of inner satisfaction and have given me the opportunity for healthy self-expression. I, too, have been blessed by faithful friends, by my mother's desire to give to others, and by her attitude of gratitude. All of this has helped to transform my tears of sadness into tears of joy.

32

Are these socks clean or dirty?

Dad built our house in 1948 – before he met Mom. Had he known he was going to marry the queen of clean, he might have thought differently about the back entrance. He might have considered a mud room, a laundry room, or some other place where we could put our shoes and socks upon entering the house. But as it was, our back door led almost immediately to the kitchen on the left, the family room on the right and the cellar steps straight ahead. So we used to line our shoes up on the ends of the cellar steps. We used to leave our socks there, too, or somewhere else on the floor. As a result, Mom used to say, "Are these socks clean or dirty?" Translation: "Why did you leave your socks where they don't belong?"

This was Mom's attempt to get us to be as organized as she was. If there is an opposite image of a pack rat, it was my mother. She kept the house neat, orderly, and devoid of clutter. She used to say, "If you don't need it, throw it away." And she did. Everything – from the dresser drawers to the spice rack, from the recipe box to the box that kept all receipts – had its place. She was constantly telling us that "if we put things where they belong, we will always be able to find them." She was so right.

Mom didn't have a computer, a mobile device, or a spreadsheet to help her stay organized. She used pen and paper. She was always writing things down so she wouldn't forget them, and she encouraged us to do the same. Her organizational skills reaped a myriad of benefits. When life brought disorder, at least the house was in order, which gave Mom a sense of calm amid the chaos. Because she was organized, she was able to be productive. She wouldn't allow clutter or small tasks to build up. Therefore, there wasn't much catching up to do. She did housework as it needed to be done and paid the bills as they needed to be paid. By staying ahead of the curve, she was able to save both money and time. Whenever we had to leave the house, she didn't have to spend time looking for her keys, her purse, her coat, her umbrella, or anything else, because she always knew where things were. As a result, she was always on time – or early. All of this made life a little easier and a lot less stressful for her and for her children.

Like my mom, being organized has helped me focus on what's important in life. For Mom, her children and her faith were at the top of the list. She made time for daily prayer and daily Mass, which in turn deepened her awareness of the most important things in life and helped her to focus on them. Perhaps this is how she had the energy to bake cookies for a friend in need at 9:00 at night. In this way, Mom showed us how being organized not only benefits ourselves, but others as well. She opened our eyes to how the simple act of picking up our dirty socks might lead us to have time and space available for others.

33

*Turn off the TV
and read a book*

As a child, I loved watching television. My
brother and I would sit in front of the TV and
watch variety programs like *The Carol Burnett
Show* or situation comedies such as *Leave it to
Beaver, The Beverly Hillbillies, Gilligan's Island,*
and *Gomer Pyle, U.S.M.C.* Whenever Mom
felt her children had too much screen time, she
would say, "Turn off the TV and read a book."
Mom was echoing a famous quote by American
author and comedian Groucho Marx, who said,
"I find television very educational. Every time
someone switches it on I go into another room
and read a good book."

My mother helped us to realize the value of
reading over watching television. But according
to statistics, most children – and adults – spend

more time watching television than reading, with devastating effect. Statistics say that Americans spend as much as 34 hours or more per week watching television – that's almost as much time as we spend at work. The preferred leisure activity in most households is watching TV, accounting for more than half of our free time. Meanwhile, the literacy statistics in the United States continue to be grim. It's estimated that nearly half the adults in the U.S. are considered functionally illiterate, which means they can't read or write well enough to do simple, everyday tasks such as balance a checkbook or read a prescription. It's no surprise that illiteracy is often linked to poverty and crime. As Mom guessed, reading is not only fundamental, it is essential to the well-being of society.

Reading exercises the mind. When we crack open a book, we engage our brains in narrative and in plot, in characters and in dialogue. These elements help our brain create new memories. That kind of mental stimulation sharpens our intellect and improves our brain-power. Curling up with a great book can help reduce stress as we temporarily surrender our cares to the imagination of the author, immersing ourselves in story, transporting ourselves to another place and time. Reading expands our vocabulary and our view of the world. Reading about other cultures and other lands can lead to a better understanding between people, cultivating empathy and solidarity. Reading fosters relationships and community by bringing people together in book clubs for social discourse. Devouring words is like digesting wisdom and light. Mom pushed, poked, and prodded us to read. Her encouragement is one of the reasons I am writing this book.

I used to make my living by working in television. These days, I rarely watch it. Thanks to Mom, I'm too busy reading – or writing.

34

Write a book

In many ways, my mother's hands told the story of her life. Mom's hands were strong and muscular from years of hard work both inside and outside the house. And they were thick-skinned. Perhaps this is how she could tolerate dishwater that was scalding. "As hot as I can stand it," she used to say. Her nails were always short – not because she couldn't grow them, but because having long nails just wasn't practical. However, her nails were usually neat and painted by her own do-it-yourself manicures. Each crevice, each vein, and each age spot seemed to tell its own tale of a woman whose hands loved to be immersed in the fullness of life, whether it was kneading dough, rolling meatballs, or being the first in the room to grab and hold a baby. The left finger of my mother's left hand was adorned with two rings, the engagement ring and the wedding ring that our father gave her. My father died in 1967. Mom never removed those rings.

In January of 1993 while Mom was recovering in the hospital from a stroke, she lost the diamond that was set in the engagement ring. She was devastated. Our attempts to find it were in vain. My brother and I decided to have the ring reset with a new stone but we waited almost a year to give it to her. It was Christmas Eve around 10:30 p.m. and we were getting ready to leave to go to midnight Mass. We received the predictable cry from Mom around that time, "C'mon, let's go, it's 11:00. We'll never get a seat!" (In order to be early, she would often tell us the wrong time so we would hurry up.) We were standing in the kitchen and we told her that we had a gift for her. My brother gave her the neatly wrapped box. When she opened it, she burst into tears of surprise and delight. Then she told us the story of how our father proposed, a story we had never heard before. Our father proposed by giving her a ring – that same ring, also on Christmas Eve, also shortly before midnight Mass.

Stories are powerful and profound. They give meaning to our lives. But stories are only effective if they are told. The more stories are told, the more they matter. No matter what life situation I found myself in, my mother would say, "Write a book." She believed I had a story to tell and she wanted me to tell it. At the time, she had no idea that I was interested in writing. "Write a book" was just one of her many sayings but she said it so often, she must have planted a seed in my brain that eventually grew into the words in front of you. My mother knew we learn from one another's stories and telling the stories of our lives, no matter how ordinary, might have an effect on someone else. In saying "Write a book," she was echoing what Martin Luther said in the 16th century: "If you want to change the world, pick up your pen and write."

So take Mom's and Luther's advice. "Write a book," tell your story, even if you have never written anything before. Who knows? You might not change the world, but you might change a life.

35

If I weren't here, would you know how to…?

It was just a routine drive to Pittsburgh to see one of my doctors, but for some reason, that trip stayed in my memory. About halfway there, my mother turned to me and said, "If I weren't here, would you know how to get to the doctor's office by yourself?" A little panic rose up inside of me. I thought, "What do you mean if you're not here? Of course you're going to be here." But deep down I realized my mother was trying to tell me that she wouldn't be around forever. She wanted to be sure I knew how to get to the place to which we had traveled countless times since I was a toddler. But more than that, she wanted to be sure that I would be OK on my own – no matter where life would take me.

There comes a time when every parent and child must part. Detachment begins when the baby is taken from the womb. It continues when children go to preschool for just a few hours. Next is grade school where children spend the entire day. Then comes the big separation, whether that be college, the military, or leaving home for a job, when young adults are sent forth to encounter the world without their parents close by. At each stage of separation, there is a bit of sadness and a bit of eager anticipation. By that time, parents hope they have given their children enough tools to deal with life as an adult.

My mother died when I was only 32 years old. A little more than three decades was not enough time to spend with her. Still, in that short time, she supplied me with the wisdom and knowledge I need to survive in this world. A lot of that wisdom came through her sayings.

Mother isn't here now. But thanks to her wise words, I know how to…

If I weren't here, would you know how to…?

Pray
Appreciate history in the making
Ask for help / carry only what I need
Be grateful
Be ready
Be at peace
Focus my attention on the things that matter
Be compassionate towards others
Be satisfied with very little
Pay attention in church and live out my
    faith in the world
Recognize the importance of our global
    community
Recognize our common humanity
Stand tall
Drive carefully and generously
Tell the truth and face the truth
Keep my mouth shut
Appreciate the opportunity to work
Take my time when doing work
Learn to do things the right way
Taste new things
Eat slowly and chew my food
Only consume what I need
Be courteous in ways big and small
Save money

Be my own consumer advocate
Let go
Live well and die well
Live in the now
Accept responsibility for my actions
Take care of myself
Find ways to deal with pain
Get and stay organized
Read
Write a book
Survive

I have been able to reap the harvest of the seeds of my mother's wisdom. Mom, your work is done. May you now reap the harvest of your good words and good deeds!

A mother holds her children's hands for just a short time, but holds their hearts forever.

Anonymous

Some of Mom's favorite recipes

Some of Mom's favorite recipes

Easter Bread

2 packages dry yeast

2½ cups warm water

1 lemon cake mix

5 cups or more of flour

2 eggs

1 teaspoon lemon flavoring

Dissolve yeast in 2½ cups warm water in a large bowl.

Add dry ingredients and mix with wooden spoon.

Beat eggs and add lemon flavoring and add both to the mix.

Knead with hands.

Let rise in bowl until double.

Divide dough into 3 parts and place in 3 bread pans buttered and floured or prepared with a non-stick spray.

Let rise again until double.

Bake at 350 for 35 minutes or until golden brown.

Brush butter on top of warm bread.

Italian Wedding Cookies (with icing)

1 stick butter, room temperature

1½ cups sugar

6 eggs beaten

1 teaspoon vanilla

½ cup milk

1 tablespoon oil

4 teaspoons baking powder

4 cups or more of flour

Cream butter and sugar, then mix in eggs, vanilla, milk and oil.

Add baking powder and flour and mix.

Cover dough and let sit for 15 minutes.

Roll dough into 1 inch balls and place on greased cookie sheet.

Bake at 350 for 15 minutes.

Icing

1 tablespoon melted butter

1 cup powdered sugar

1 tablespoon or more of water to thin

1 drop of your choice of food coloring

Some of Mom's favorite recipes

Apple Squares

1½ cups sugar

⅔ cup vegetable oil

1 teaspoon cinnamon

1 teaspoon nutmeg

1 teaspoon cloves

½ teaspoon salt

1½ teaspoons baking soda diluted in ½ cup of hot water, then add ½ cup of cool water.

3 cups flour

2½ cups diced apples

1½ cups raisins

1 cup chopped walnuts

Mix all ingredients and spread in a greased cookie sheet.

Bake at 375 for 25-30 minutes.

When the cake has cooled, ice with maple icing or an icing of your choice.

Cut into squares.

Coconut Birds Nests/Thumbprints

½ cup butter

⅓ cup sugar

1 cup flour

1 egg

½ teaspoon vanilla

¾ cup coconut

Mix butter and sugar. Add flour and mix. Add egg yolk and vanilla.

Roll dough into 1 inch balls. Dip balls into egg white, then roll in coconut.

Indent the center of the ball with your thumb to make room for filling.

Bake on greased cookie sheet for 25 minutes at 300 degrees or until lightly browned.

When cookies are cool, add filling – apricot, strawberry preserves or filling of your choice.